DI025173

lemonade

50 COOL RECIPES
FOR CLASSIC,
FLAVORED, AND
HARD LEMONADES
AND SPARKLERS

FRED THOMPSON

THE HARVARD COMMON PRESS
BOSTON, MASSACHUSETTS

In Dad's memory and for Mom's support

THE HARVARD COMMON PRESS
535 Albany Street
Boston, Massachusetts 02118
www.harvardcommonpress.com

Text ©2002 by Fred Thompson
Recipe Photographs ©2002 by Susan Byrnes
Photographs on pages 8, 15, 16, 28, 48, 58, and 72 ©2002 by PhotoDisc

Printed in China
Printed on acid-free paper

Library of Congress Cataloging-in-Publication Data

Thompson, Fred
    Lemonade : 50 cool recipes for classic, flavored, and hard lemonades and sparklers / by
Fred Thompson
    p. cm.
    ISBN 1-55832-229-9 (cl : alk. paper)
    1. Lemonade. I. Title.
TX817.L45 T456 2002
641.8'75–dc21

                                                                            2001051601

ISBN-13: 978-1-55832-229-5
ISBN-10: 1-55832-229-9

10 9 8 7 6 5

Jacket and interior design by Elizabeth Van Itallie

Jacket recipe: Frozen Lemonade, page 26

contents

do you stop at all lemonade stands? Don't you remember your first lemonade stand, or your kid's, or your grandchild's? It was your first entrepreneurial experience. What a feeling of accomplishment when you made a sale! What a sense of anticipation as each car approached! Did you drink more than you sold? And no matter if you did, Mom was always there with a fresh pitcher when your inventory got low. Oh, sure, part of the fun was squeezing the lemons and generally making a mess in the kitchen, but the true excitement came while you were standing at that lemonade stand.

My mom helped make signs, gave me "change money," and usually had a batch of cookies to encourage my enthusiasm. Doesn't that sound like your mother, too? Dad was not to be left out: he would always buy the remaining inventory at day's end, making certain that it appeared that a profit had been made. If it was a Saturday, he would make his special limeade to celebrate our success as true business people. I have included that limeade recipe in memory of my father and just because it tastes darn good.

Then there were the trips to my grandmother's rural house, where she made lemonade in a galvanized washtub. Maybe it was the well water or the fact that all my uncles and aunts and cousins came to dip from that tub, but lemonade at Grandmother's was always the best. Had I known that this book was in my future, I would have paid closer attention to how she made her lemonade. I suspect that it was her hands and eyes that told her how hard to roll the lemons and how much sugar and water was needed. I'm sure she didn't use a recipe.

The cycle has been repeated many times. One of the few times my sister and I were not at each other's throats was at our lemonade stand. And as a father, I cherish the memories of helping my daughter with her many lemonade stands in her early years. Lemonade binds us together in a way that few things do. It is part of our American soul. And now we have found that lemonade is not just for the summer months but is a year-round beverage. Lemonade has gone upscale, with restaurants, bars, and caterers all trying to outdo each other with the latest permutation of flavors to blend with lemonade. The raging debate over the balance of sweet to sour has become as personal as our religion.

Religion had quite the role in the evolution of lemonade. The lemon is native to Asia, but by the time of the Crusades, it had spread into the rugged terrain of the Middle East. The Christian warriors brought the lemon back with them from their campaigns, leaving a trail of seeds throughout Europe. And Christopher Columbus gets the credit for bringing the lemon to the New World.

History gets fuzzy on exactly when and where the first lemonade was made. One camp believes that Queen Isabella served Columbus lemonade when he approached her about financing his voyage. Others put lemonade's beginnings in Paris in the 1600s, when a sharp drop in the price of sugar encouraged people to use it in new ways, and lemonade was born. It was, however, a French immigrant, living in Philadelphia, who first mixed carbonated water with lemonade in the 1830s.

In the twenty-first century, lemonade has become the victim of our ever-quickening pace. Powdered "belly wash," reconstituted lemon juice, and canned versions of lemonade have replaced real lemonade, with all its therapeutic benefits: squeezing the lemons, waiting for the sugar syrup to cool, and having friends and family to share this thirst-quenching treat. Have you stopped at a lemonade stand today?

the
basics

Not everything about making lemonade is obvious. Here is a short but
helpful chapter on buying, juicing,
and storing lemons, along with some
general lemon stuff. Also included
are serving suggestions and how to
improve on store-bought powdered
mixes and frozen concentrates.

Buying lemons is an exercise in confusion. Are the bigger 2-for-99-cent lemons juicier than the smaller 9-in-a-bag lemons for $2.49? With lemons, bigger or more expensive is not necessarily better. Look for lemons with a smooth skin and no blemishes. They should feel heavy for their size. The medium-size, by-the-bag lemons tend to have thinner rinds than the bigger ones. That makes them easier to juice and makes for better-looking slices and wedges for garnishes. Lemons that feel rock hard usually have thicker rinds; if you have a choice, avoid them.

Lemons have a pretty good life expectancy. In your refrigerator, they will last for several weeks; at room temperature, about a week. Of course, there are variables, such as the season and how far those lemons had to travel. Lemonade has a refrigerator shelf life of about a week. Those made with fresh fruit purees should be consumed in three days or so. In either case, I doubt they'll hang around that long.

Never use reconstituted lemon juice to make lemonade. It bears absolutely no resemblance to freshly squeezed juice. If lemons are ridiculously expensive or don't look so good, you can always use frozen juice. Lemon juice does freeze well, so when you spot a good price on lemons, buy lots of them, then juice them and freeze the juice in 1-cup containers. The frozen juice will last up to a year and probably will save you some money in the middle of lemonade season. Alternatively, you can buy frozen juice (not concentrate) in a 7.5-ounce bottle, which conveniently yields just shy of a cup.

Most of the refrigerated supermarket lemonades are okay, as long as you stick to the national brands. I found that by adding the juice of 2 lemons, their rinds, and ¼ cup sugar per 64 ounces of lemonade, I could really ratchet up the flavor. In a pinch, when making blended or flavored lemonades, with the noted additions, these products will supply a pleasurable result.

Frozen lemonade and limeade concentrates are used throughout this book. They can give you quick, intense flavor when you're making flavored lemonades. With a little fresh lemon juice and sugar, these products also make passable lemonade.

Powdered lemonade mixes and cheap gallons of premade lemonade are known as "belly wash" in the trade for their lack of substance. Adding ½ cup fresh lemon juice, lemon rinds, and some sugar to powdered products (especially Country Time) cuts some of the artificial flavor if you are patient and let all the ingredients mellow in the refrigerator for a couple of hours.

Many of the recipes call for using the zest of the lemon. That is the intense yellow skin, and it is filled with flavorful oils. When "grated zest" is called for, simply use the smallest holes on a cheese grater or one of those handy new microplane zesters, being careful not to include the white part of the rind, which can be bitter. If strips of zest are needed, use your vegetable peeler to carefully peel the yellow skin from the lemon. I find that Y-shaped vegetable peelers work best on all citrus fruits. For flavor or garnish, you can use a zesting tool to make thin, short pieces of zest. I know this might seem obvious, but zest the lemons before you juice them.

Please do note that I was born in the South, where we like things sweet. To me, good lemonade starts sweet and leaves tart, and in between are all the intricacies that make lemonade great. My taste buds may not be the same as yours. In addition, the tartness of the fruit varies from day to day, so expect to make adjustments in sweetness. You are making this for you, not me.

You might be surprised to see salt listed in many of the recipes. A small amount of salt will bring out the flavor, both sweet and tart. Remember this if you get a batch of weak lemons—and use only kosher salt.

sugar syrup, basic and otherwise

Several recipes in this book call for sugar syrup, and the directions may vary depending on the specific recipe. Sugar syrup keeps for a week at room temperature and about a month refrigerated. Having some on hand speeds up the process of making fresh lemonade. A friend, Ann Robeson, and her sister, Boo (really), have a lemonade stand at the Pumpkin Festival in Spring Hope, North Carolina. Their sugar syrup recipe calls for 5 gallons of water and 5 pounds plus $1\frac{1}{2}$ cups of sugar. That makes a lot of sugar syrup, and it allows the sisters to have the very freshest lemonade for their customers. Sugar syrup also is used in many cocktails, for sweetening iced tea, or to lend an interesting flavor to any beverage that requires a sweet note.

1 cup water
$1\frac{1}{2}$ cups granulated sugar

1. Combine the water and sugar in a small saucepan. Bring to a gentle boil over medium heat, stirring until the sugar is dissolved.

2. Remove from the heat and let cool completely. Store in an airtight container in the refrigerator.

➤ MAKES ABOUT 2 CUPS

MINT SYRUP Add $\frac{1}{2}$ cup coarsely chopped fresh mint leaves to the saucepan and proceed with the recipe. Depending on the strength of the mint flavor you want, either strain the syrup at the end of the cooking or, for a stronger mint flavor, leave the mint in the saucepan until the syrup is cool and then strain.

GINGER SYRUP Add 5 quarter-size slices of fresh ginger to the saucepan and proceed as directed. Let the sugar syrup cool, then strain out the ginger.

ORANGE, LEMON, OR LIME SYRUP Add the grated zest of 2 oranges, 2 lemons, or 2 limes to the saucepan and proceed as directed. Let the sugar syrup cool, then strain out the zest.

HERB SYRUP Thyme, rosemary, and bay leaves all add interest to sugar syrup. Start with about 3 sprigs fresh thyme, 1 sprig fresh rosemary, or a couple of bay leaves. Add them to the saucepan and proceed as directed. Let the herb steep in the cooling syrup for 5 minutes, then check for depth of flavor. Continue to steep until the desired level of flavor is achieved, but no longer than 30 minutes, then strain out the herb. Herb syrup should be used within a week, as it tends to get bitter if stored any longer.

how to squeeze a lemon

First, all citrus fruits will release more juice when at room temperature. Rolling each piece of fruit on your countertop also will increase the amount of juice and release some of the oils in the rind, which is packed with flavor. Lemons also can be microwaved on high for 10 to 20 seconds, which helps to release even more juice or to bring up the temperature of cold lemons in a hurry. However, boiling water poured over lemon juice presents a different problem. Some recipes (not in this book) call for boiling water. The hot water dissipates the natural vitamins and other healthy stuff in lemon juice. Please note that the water in my recipes is always cool, and sugar syrups and other additions are cooled before adding them to the lemon juice.

You do not need an expensive juicer to have fun making lemonade. The old glass reamer works just fine. I do like the Mexican lime press that turns limes inside out. There are several electric reamers on the market for $20 or so, which can save your muscles if you plan to make a lot of lemonade or get hooked on freshly squeezed orange juice. I have used the citrus attachment for my KitchenAid stand mixer and have been very pleased. I also have used the basic citrus reamer powered by *moi*.

How many lemons equal how much juice? I find that 6 medium-size lemons yield 1 cup of juice. Eight limes yield 1 cup of juice. But to save time and stress, always pick up at least 2 extra lemons or limes at the store. You can always use them as garnish. And remember to strain the seeds out of your lemon juice.

serving lemonade

I like lemonade served in tall glasses. My personal favorite is a collins glass. However, I have had lemonade in Mason jars and paper cups that tasted just as good as any from a glass, so don't get caught up in having a set of lemon-ade-only glasses.

Nothing is more fanciful than a round bowl-shaped pitcher—the kind in Kool-Aid ads, with the face drawn in the condensation. Filled with lemonade, lemon slices, and mint, it is a picture of pure refreshment. Plastic containers or even recycled juice jars also work fine. Just use a vessel with a mouth large enough to get a stirring spoon in there or one with a tight lid that won't leak when you shake it. Keep any garnishes consistent with the ingredients in the lemonade. Remember, a wedge or slice of lemon always works, and mint tends to enhance the experience of most lemonades, making it a good choice as well.

This book was a blast to do. It is in no way intended to be the last or most authoritative work on the subject. I hope that I have given you recipes that you'll enjoy. But most of all, I hope that you will use this book to get your creative juices flowing. Play with lemonade. Please make some from scratch. There is a lot of truth to the cliché "When life gives you lemons, make lemonade."

the old-fashioned way

You have to start somewhere, and these recipes are classic ways of making lemonade. All of them go about transforming lemon juice, water, and sugar into a refreshing treat. I think one or more will become your favorite ways to make fresh, great-tasting lemonade.

lemonade
concentrate

There may be more than a million ways to make lemonade, and some recipes are fussier than others. This one takes a straightforward approach. Make a base, keep it refrigerated, and you can make yourself a single glass or an entire pitcher. I've even frozen this concentrate in January, when the price of lemons sometimes drops, and used it in July with no problems.

2 cups granulated sugar

4 cups water

2 cups freshly squeezed lemon juice (about 12 lemons)

1. In a 2-quart saucepan, combine the sugar and water. Bring to a boil over medium heat, stirring to dissolve the sugar. Reduce the heat to a simmer and cook for about 3 minutes. Remove from the heat and let cool completely.

2. Pour the sugar syrup into a 1½-quart container and stir in the lemon juice. Refrigerate, covered, until cold. It will keep for about 2 weeks in the refrigerator or for several months, in a tightly covered plastic container, in the freezer.

3. To serve by the glass or the pitcher, combine equal parts lemonade concentrate and water, sparkling water, or club soda.

➤ MAKES 5 CUPS CONCENTRATE, WHICH WILL YIELD ABOUT 10 SERVINGS

scratch lemonade

This is basic, no-fuss lemonade. The hardest part is juicing the lemons and limes. The small amount of lime juice rounds out the lemonade, making it more invigorating. Be sure to put the lemon rinds in the lemonade, because while you were juicing the lemons, you were also breaking loose some of the oils in the rinds, which have mountains of flavor.

6 cups cold water

1 1/2 to 2 cups granulated sugar, more or less according to your "pucker factor"

2 cups freshly squeezed lemon juice (about 12 lemons), rinds reserved

1/4 cup freshly squeezed lime juice (about 2 limes)

1. In a 2 1/2-quart container, combine the water and sugar, stirring until the sugar is dissolved. Add the lemon and lime juices and stir once more. Throw in the lemon rinds.

2. Chill until very cold and serve over ice.

➤ MAKES 2 QUARTS

To make pink lemonade, you can add grenadine, cranberry juice cocktail, or red food coloring until a nice pink hue develops.

old-fashioned lemonade

Homemade lemonade is comfort food. Like Mom's meat loaf or mashed potatoes, the memories we associate with lemonade are special. Homemade lemonade is a treasure we need to pass on. My daughter, Laura, suggested that since the rind has lots of flavor (actually lemon oils), I needed to get it in the lemonade somehow. Since she was one of my chief guinea pig tasters, I gave it some thought, and here's the result. By infusing the zest into the sugar syrup, I got a bigger and more stimulating lemon essence, which made the lemonade better.

SUGAR SYRUP

Grated zest of 2 lemons
2 cups granulated sugar
2 cups water

LEMONADE

2 cups freshly squeezed lemon juice (about 12 lemons), 5 or 6 of
   the rinds reserved and roughly chopped
3 cups cold water
Lemon slices for garnish (optional)

1. To make the sugar syrup, combine the zest, sugar, and water in a medium-size saucepan. Bring to a gentle boil over medium heat, stirring to dissolve the sugar. Remove from the heat, cover, and let steep for 15 minutes.

2. To make the lemonade, pour the sugar syrup into a 2-quart container. Let cool, then add the lemon juice, chopped lemon rinds, and cold water. Stir well to combine.

3. Chill until very cold. Serve over ice, garnished with lemon slices if desired.

➤ MAKES A LITTLE SHY OF 2 QUARTS

The lemon zest-infused sugar syrup is an elegant way to sweeten and add lemon flavor to iced tea. Set out a small pitcher the next time you serve iced tea.

wooden tub lemonade

My paternal grandmother's family had a reunion every September. An old community building would be filled with long tables, burdened with platters and bowls overflowing with food. After I would sneak a piece of my aunt's cornbread, I would bolt for a huge wooden tub full of homemade lemonade. It was the elixir of the gods. Reconfigured here in a more manageable size, this recipe is the lemonade of my boyhood.

8 to 10 lemons. at room temperature
1 to 2 cups granulated sugar. to your taste
Cold water. as needed

1. Roll the lemons on your countertop to break the membranes. Juice the lemons until you have $1\frac{1}{2}$ cups and pour that into a 1-gallon container. Add the lemon rinds, then pour the sugar over the rinds and juice (1 cup for tart, $1\frac{1}{2}$ cups for medium tart, and 2 cups if you like it on the sweet side). Let macerate for 1 hour at room temperature.

2. Add enough cold water to fill the container.

3. Chill until very cold and serve over ice.

➤ MAKES 1 GALLON

Rolling the lemons is important to maximize the amount of juice released and extricate the oils contained in the rinds.

Lemons can be microwaved for 10 to 20 seconds. which increases their temperature and thus releases more juice.

summer blahs
lemonade

Don't you just hate summer colds? Have you noticed that when you have one, nobody else does? You need sympathy. You need a treat that's good and soothing. Try this lemonade when the need arises, or just because you like honey.

1 cup honey
9 cups cold water
1 cup freshly squeezed lemon juice (about 6 lemons)

1. In a small saucepan, combine the honey and 1 cup of the water. Place over medium heat and stir until homogenized, 3 to 5 minutes. Remove from the heat and let cool.

2. In a 1½-quart container, blend the honey syrup, lemon juice, and remaining 8 cups water.

3. Chill until very cold and serve over ice.

➤ MAKES 1½ QUARTS

If you are a honey fan or feel that it is healthier than regular sugar, give it a shot in other lemonade recipes in place of the sugar called for in the sugar syrup.

tea-monade

I've been drinking this combination for a long time. Now even the national brands are jumping in with their versions. You can make Tea-monade in any proportions you like: half-and-half, three to one, whatever strikes your fancy. I understand that in some golf course grill rooms, when you order a Jack Nicklaus, this is what you get.

TEA
4 cups cold water
3 regular-size tea bags
$1/2$ cup granulated sugar

LEMONADE
2 cups Lemonade Concentrate (page 18)
2 cups cold water

1. To make the tea, in a small saucepan, bring 2 cups of the water to a boil and add the tea bags. Remove from the heat, cover, and let steep for 15 minutes.

2. Remove the tea bags and add the sugar, stirring to dissolve. Stir in the remaining 2 cups water, pour into a 1-quart container, and chill until very cold.

3. To make the lemonade, mix the lemonade concentrate and cold water together in a 1-quart container and chill until very cold.

4. To serve, blend the tea and lemonade together by the glass to your liking. I recommend half tea, half lemonade. Serve over ice.

➤ MAKES 2 QUARTS

frozen lemonade

This is a fun drink to make with the kids. It's almost like drinking a lemonade granita. Of course, this drink can "grow up" with the addition of rum, tequila, or vodka.

1 cup freshly squeezed lemon juice (about 6 lemons)
1 cup granulated sugar
4 cups cold water (approximately)
1 cup cracked ice (approximately)
6 maraschino cherries with stems for garnish (optional)

1. In a blender, process the lemon juice and sugar for 30 seconds to mix well. Add 2 cups of the water and half the ice and blend, crushing the ice. Add the remaining ice and water. (If this stretches the limits of your blender, add less ice and water.) Blend on high speed until the mixture becomes a frozen concoction.

2. Divide among 6 glasses and top each with a cherry.

➤ MAKES 6 SERVINGS

Use caution when making this lemonade. Don't overestimate your blender's strength or capacity. If you need to, divide the ingredients in half and make it in two batches.

mediterranean-style lemonade

An Italian, a Sicilian, and a Turk all described lemonades like this one to me. This lemonade is much drier and tarter than most in this book.

4 cups cold water

$1/2$ cup granulated sugar

Zest of 1 lemon, taken off in long, thin strips

$1/2$ cup freshly squeezed lemon juice (about 3 lemons)

1. Combine 2 cups of the water and the sugar in a medium-size saucepan and bring to a gentle boil over medium heat, stirring to dissolve the sugar. Reduce the heat to medium-low, add the zest, and simmer for 2 minutes. Remove from the heat, cover, and let steep for 15 minutes. Strain out the zest with a fine-mesh strainer, if desired.

2. In a $1^1/_2$-quart container, combine the lemon-flavored syrup, lemon juice, and remaining 2 cups water.

3. Chill until very cold and serve over ice.

➤ MAKES ABOUT 1 QUART

When removing the zest of the lemon, or any citrus fruit, try to avoid the white pith, which can be bitter.

fruit-
seduced
lemonade

Lemonade loves company, making it very amenable to experimentation with other fruits. Great chefs for centuries and from around the world have been using the acid in lemons to heighten and brighten other flavors. When you mix lemons with other fruits, you get the best of both. The recipes in this chapter are starting points. Don't be afraid to mix two together for your own special blend of fruit-seduced lemonade. Hint: try combining the raspberry and mango lemonades. Have fun.

strawberry– rhubarb lemonade

Intensely bitter, rhubarb becomes a willing partner when blended with straw-berries and sugar. Nothing announces the arrival of spring more potently than strawberries and rhubarb. With this recipe, you can get a jump on summer by combining these seasonal gems with lemon.

4 cups cold water

3 stalks rhubarb, trimmed and cut into large dice (about 2 cups)

1 cup granulated sugar, or to taste

Zest of 1 lemon

$1/4$ teaspoon kosher salt

1 cup hulled and quartered fresh strawberries

1 teaspoon pure vanilla extract

1 cup freshly squeezed lemon juice (about 6 lemons)

1 cup hulled and sliced fresh strawberries

1. In a 3-quart saucepan, combine the water, rhubarb, sugar, zest, and salt. Bring to a boil, stirring occasionally, until the sugar is dissolved. Reduce the heat to a simmer, cover, and cook until the rhubarb is soft, about 10 min-utes. Add the quartered strawberries and cook for 4 minutes more. Remove from the heat and let cool for 15 minutes.

2. Strain the fruit mixture through a fine-mesh strainer into a 2-quart con-tainer, pushing down on the solids to extract as much juice as possible. Add the vanilla and lemon juice and stir to combine. Let cool completely, then chill until very cold.

3. When ready to serve, add the sliced strawberries and serve over ice.

➤ MAKES 1½ QUARTS

Rhubarb is technically a vegetable, but it is almost always used in some fruitlike concoction. Look for bright red, firm stalks. Do not use the leaves; they can be toxic.

raspberry lemonade

Folks the world over seem to have a passion for raspberries. This naturally sweet-tart fruit lends itself supremely to partnering with lemonade.

2 pints fresh raspberries or one 12-ounce bag frozen raspberries
   (not in syrup)
1 cup granulated sugar
2 cups freshly squeezed lemon juice (about 12 lemons)
4 cups cold water

1. In a food processor or blender, pulse the raspberries and sugar until smooth.

2. Strain the puree through a fine-mesh strainer into a 1¹/₂-quart container, pressing on the solids to get all of the juice. Add the lemon juice and water and stir until blended.

3. Chill until very cold and serve over ice.

➤ MAKES 1¹/₂ QUARTS

blackberry lemonade

Down South, blackberries grow wild. After strawberries, blueberries and black-berries are Southerners' favorite fruits. Like raspberries, blackberries have a sweet-tart flavor.

2 pints fresh blackberries
1 cup granulated sugar
2 cups freshly squeezed lemon juice (about 12 lemons)
3 cups cold water

1. In a food processor or blender, pulse the blackberries and sugar until smooth. Strain the puree into a 1½-quart container, pressing on the solids to get all of the juice. Stir in the lemon juice and water until well blended.

2. Chill until very cold and serve over ice.

➤ MAKES 1½ QUARTS

57th street blue-berry lemonade

Fifty-Seventh Street in New York City is most widely associated with designer clothing stores and CBS. It is also home to the Four Seasons Hotel. I had blueberry lemonade there when a flavored-lemonade obsession gripped the city. This is my attempt to replicate that tasty treat.

2 cups fresh blueberries, picked over for stems

$^1/_2$ to $^3/_4$ cup granulated sugar, depending on the sweetness of the blueberries

1 cup freshly squeezed lemon juice (about 6 lemons)

2 cups cold water

Superfine sugar, if needed

1. Taste one of the blueberries to determine its sweetness. In a blender or food processor, process the blueberries and granulated sugar until smooth. Strain the puree through a fine-mesh strainer into a medium-size bowl, stirring and pushing on the puree to get all the juice.

2. Pour the blueberry juice into a 1-quart container. Add the lemon juice and water and stir or shake to combine. Check for sweetness, adding superfine sugar to taste, if needed.

3. Chill until very cold and serve over ice.

➤ MAKES 1 QUART

tailgate spiced cranberry lemonade

This fall lemonade is a definite winner for those still-balmy days of early football season. It is tarter and more bracing than others and offers an adult taste. You, of course, can add more sugar, if needed. So grab a chicken wing and a glass of this splendid lemonade.

10 cloves

2 cinnamon sticks, each about 3 inches long

4 cups cold water

2 cups cranberry juice cocktail

$1/3$ cup granulated sugar

One 12-ounce can frozen lemonade concentrate, thawed

1. In a medium-size saucepan, combine the cloves, cinnamon, 2 cups of the water, cranberry juice, and sugar. Bring to a boil, stirring until the sugar is dissolved. Remove from the heat.

2. Strain the mixture through a fine-mesh strainer into a 2-quart container. Add the lemonade concentrate and remaining 2 cups water and stir to blend well.

3. Chill until very cold and serve over ice.

➤ MAKES 2 QUARTS

drugstore citrusade

Before *Cheers,* everybody knew your name at the drugstore. That's where you could get the best chicken salad or grilled cheese sandwich. And there was always a citrus fountain drink to enjoy along with your lunch. At one time, I had a catering business and a small grill. We sold tons of this citrusade.

SYRUP

2 1/2 cups water

2 cups granulated sugar

1 cup freshly squeezed lemon juice (about 6 lemons)

2/3 cup freshly squeezed orange juice

Grated zest of 1 orange

TO SERVE

Cold water, as needed

Lemon and orange slices for garnish (optional)

1. To make the syrup, combine the water and sugar in a small saucepan. Bring to a gentle boil over medium heat, stirring to dissolve the sugar. Reduce the heat to a low simmer and cook for no more than 5 minutes. Remove from the heat and let cool.

2. In a 1-quart container, combine the lemon juice, orange juice, and zest. Stir in the cooled sugar syrup and let the mixture sit at room temperature for 2 hours, then chill until very cold.

3. To serve, fill a 10-ounce glass with ice (cracked or crushed is best). Put 1/3 to 1/2 cup of the syrup (to your taste) in the glass, then top off with cold water. Garnish with an orange or lemon slice, if desired.

➤ MAKES 1 QUART SYRUP, WHICH WILL YIELD ABOUT 8 SERVINGS

You could use sparkling water or club soda for a more effervescent beverage. If you would like to serve this by the pitcher, mix 2 cups cold water with all the syrup and adjust the flavor from that point, adding more water if necessary.

strawberry lemonade

Strawberries and lemonade—enough said? The combination of these two fruits is a match made in lemonade heaven.

2 pints fresh strawberries, hulled and cut in half

1 1/2 cups granulated sugar

3 cups cold water

1 1/2 cups freshly squeezed lemon juice (about 9 lemons)

1. In a food processor or blender, process the strawberries and sugar until smooth.

2. Combine the strawberry puree, water, and lemon juice in a 2-quart container and stir to blend the flavors.

3. Chill until very cold and serve over ice.

➤ MAKES 1 1/2 QUARTS

pink apple lemonade

This colorful and different lemonade is the perfect choice for a Fourth of July celebration. The lime juice adds an intriguing flavor. Let that be your secret.

One 48-ounce bottle cranberry juice cocktail
4 cups apple juice
One 12-ounce can frozen lemonade concentrate, thawed
1/2 cup water
1/4 cup freshly squeezed lime juice (about 2 limes)
Cracked ice

1. Combine the cranberry juice cocktail, apple juice, and lemonade concentrate in a 3-quart container. Stir to blend. Add the water and lime juice and stir again.

2. Chill until very cold and serve over cracked ice.

➤ MAKES 3 QUARTS

guava lemonade

Some things should be simple, and this one's a no-brainer. It is the best pink lemonade you'll ever taste.

One 11.5-ounce can guava nectar
2 quarts freshly made, reconstituted frozen concentrate or
   store-bought refrigerated lemonade

1. Place the guava nectar in a 2 1/2-quart container. Stir in the lemonade to blend.

2. Chill until very cold and serve over ice.

➤ MAKES SLIGHTLY LESS THAN 2 1/2 QUARTS

apple lemonade

Instead of comparing apples to lemons and arguing over each one's good points, let's combine them for a lemonade sure to please all.

$^1/_2$ cup granulated sugar

$^1/_2$ cup water

$2^1/_2$ cups apple juice

1 cup freshly squeezed lemon juice (about 6 lemons)

1. Combine the sugar and water in a small saucepan and bring to a boil over medium heat, stirring until the sugar is dissolved. Remove from the heat and let cool to room temperature.

2. In a 1-quart container, combine the cooled syrup, apple juice, and lemon juice until well combined.

3. Chill until very cold and serve over ice.

➤ MAKES 1 QUART

smooth mango lemonade

It is a shame that mangoes have only recently become widely available. They have a rich, peachlike flavor and flesh that almost caress your mouth. This lemonade, for me, is better when the puree is not strained out. The texture is smooth and adds to the appeal of this golden elixir. A word of caution: if you use a blender to make your puree, do it in two batches. When selecting your mangoes, make sure they are fragrant and yield slightly to the touch.

3 large ripe mangoes
$1/2$ cup granulated sugar
2 tablespoons Rose's lime juice
$2 1/2$ cups cold water
1 cup freshly squeezed lemon juice (about 6 lemons)

1. Peel the mangoes and cut the flesh from around the pits. Chop the flesh coarsely and place in a food processor or blender. Pour the sugar over the mangoes, add the lime juice, and process until smooth, about 1 minute.

2. Pour the mango puree into a $1 1/2$-quart container. Stir in the water and lemon juice until well combined. Strain through a fine-mesh strainer, if desired.

3. Chill until very cold and serve over ice.

➤ MAKES 1 $1/2$ QUARTS (SOMEWHAT LESS IF STRAINED)

The water in this recipe can be replaced with sparkling water, club soda, or even a fruity white wine.

piña colada lemonade

A taste of the tropics and a definite "hammock" beverage to reward yourself after a long day in the yard. This one's easy once you've bought the ingredients. Oh, a shot of dark or coconut-flavored rum will make it even more relaxing.

2 quarts store-bought refrigerated lemonade
$^{1}/_{3}$ cup freshly squeezed lemon juice (about 2 lemons)
2 cups pineapple-coconut juice
$^{1}/_{4}$ cup freshly squeezed lime juice (about 2 limes)

1. In a 3-quart container, combine the lemonade and lemon juice until well blended. Taste; the lemonade should have a fresher flavor. Add the pineapple-coconut juice and lime juice and stir.

2. Chill until very cold and serve over ice.

➤ MAKES A LITTLE MORE THAN 2 $^{1}/_{2}$ QUARTS

Pineapple-coconut juice can be found in the organic section of large supermarkets and health food stores. It is also a good base for a true piña colada.

hawaiian lemonade

Some government official was on the ball when the United States allowed Hawaii to join the Union. We got a military outpost, a super honeymoon resort, and all the pineapple we can eat. The supersweet pineapple is especially tasty and the better type to use in this lemonade. Most grocery stores now have the ability to peel and core pineapples, so let them do the hard part of this recipe. Please, no canned stuff.

3 cups peeled and cored fresh pineapple cut into 1-inch chunks
$^{1}/_{2}$ cup granulated sugar
4 cups cold water
1 cup freshly squeezed lemon juice (about 6 lemons)
Fresh mint leaves for garnish (optional)

1. In a food processor or blender, pulse the pineapple and sugar a few times, then process until very smooth.

2. Combine the water and lemon juice in a 2-quart container. Strain the pineapple puree through a fine mesh strainer, if desired, or pour the puree directly into the container. Stir well to combine.

3. Chill until very cold. Serve over ice, garnished with a mint leaf if desired.

➤ MAKES 2 QUARTS

spearmint-pineapple lemonade

Fresh mint, especially spearmint, is a treat in any number of dishes. Blended here with pineapple juice, it gives a new twist to lemonade. The mint syrup from this recipe is also good for sweetening iced tea or mint juleps.

1 cup granulated sugar

1 cup water

$1/3$ cup chopped fresh spearmint leaves

One 46-ounce can pineapple juice

1 cup freshly squeezed lemon juice (about 6 lemons)

1. In a small saucepan, combine the sugar, water, and spearmint. Bring to a boil, remove from the heat, and let stand for 15 to 20 minutes to allow the mint to infuse the sugar syrup. Strain the mint-infused syrup through a fine-mesh strainer. Let cool for another 10 minutes.

2. In a $2^{1}/_{2}$-quart container, combine the pineapple juice and lemon juice. Add the mint syrup and stir to combine.

3. Chill until very cold and serve over ice.

➤ MAKES 2 QUARTS

watermelon lemonade

As the pickup truck filled with watermelons traveled down the road, my dad would always say, "There goes a load of August hams." In eastern North Carolina, watermelons carried that nickname because of their shape and harvest time. Watermelon is one of my favorite fruits. Lately, the news from the health circles is that watermelons have extra-good stuff in them. Combining two of summer's favorites, watermelon and lemonade, seems only natural.

8 cups seeded watermelon cut into 1-inch chunks
1 cup hulled and quartered fresh strawberries
1 cup granulated sugar
$1/2$ cup freshly squeezed lemon juice (about 3 lemons)
2 cups water (approximately)
Thin watermelon wedges with the rind (optional)

1. In a food processor fitted with a steel blade, pulse the watermelon, strawberries, and sugar until blended and smooth.

2. Strain through a fine-mesh strainer into a 2-quart container, pushing down on the solids to get all the juice. Add the lemon juice and enough of the water to make 1½ quarts.

3. Chill until very cold. Serve over ice with a wedge of watermelon, if desired.

➤ MAKES ABOUT 1½ QUARTS

accidental or three-juice lemonade

This is one of those food accidents. Clearing away a day's worth of lemonade testing, I had a small amount of three juices left. This is the surprisingly satisfying result. The best part is that it is so simple.

$^1/_3$ cup freshly squeezed lemon juice (about 2 lemons)
$^1/_3$ cup freshly squeezed lime juice (about 2 $^1/_2$ limes)
$^1/_3$ cup freshly squeezed orange juice
1 cup granulated sugar
$^1/_4$ teaspoon kosher salt
5 cups cold water (approximately)
Citrus slices for garnish (optional)

1. Pour the juices into a 2-quart container. Add the sugar and salt and shake or whisk to combine. Add cold water to fill the container and shake or stir until the sugar is dissolved.

2. Chill until very cold. Serve over ice, garnished with citrus slices if desired.

➤ MAKES 1 $^1/_2$ QUARTS

almond and lime lemonade

In the mountains of eastern Tennessee is the Little Greenbrier Lodge Bed & Breakfast. Everywhere I researched lemonade recipes, its Tropic Lemonade showed up. This is my inspired version of that lemonade.

4 cups cold water

One 12-ounce can frozen lemonade concentrate, thawed

One 6-ounce can frozen orange juice concentrate, thawed

Two 6-ounce cans pineapple juice

$^1/_4$ cup freshly squeezed lime juice (about 2 limes)

1 teaspoon pure vanilla extract

1 teaspoon pure almond extract

1. In a 2-quart container, combine the water, lemonade and orange juice concentrates, pineapple juice, lime juice, vanilla, and almond extract until completely blended.

2. Chill until very cold and serve over ice.

➤ MAKES ALMOST 2 QUARTS

sparkling
lemonade

The practice of blending carbonated water and lemon juice goes back to the 1800s. These lemonades make great predinner or party drinks that everyone can enjoy. Some are visually stunning, and all are cooling and refreshing. Feel free to change the carbonated component to suit your tastes and needs. All can be made into a more adult version with the addition of your favorite libation.

lime and lemonade cooler

We seem to love that lemon-and-lime combination. In this recipe, the outer limits of that medley are tested. The result? Refreshment.

5 cups water
1 1/2 cups granulated sugar
1 cup freshly squeezed lemon juice (about 6 lemons)
One 6-ounce can frozen limeade concentrate, thawed
Chilled lemon-lime soda, as needed

1. Combine the water and sugar in a 2-quart saucepan. Bring to a boil over medium heat, stirring to dissolve the sugar. Remove from the heat and let cool.

2. Pour the lemon juice and limeade concentrate into a 2-quart container. Stir in the sugar syrup until well combined and chill well.

3. To serve, fill a glass with ice and add about ½ cup of the lemon-lime mixture. Top off with the lemon-lime soda.

➤ MAKES ABOUT 2½ QUARTS

To serve this as a punch, pour all of the lemon-lime mixture into a punch bowl, add one 1-liter bottle of lemon-lime soda just before serving, and mix until well combined.

cran-orange lemonade

Easy to make, Cran-Orange Lemonade is a good choice for entertaining. You can make the base ahead, then relax. Your guests get a fresh, sparkling cocktail. It also travels well, making it a natural for picnics.

One 32-ounce bottle cranberry juice cocktail

1 cup freshly squeezed lemon juice (about 6 lemons)

$1/2$ cup freshly squeezed orange juice

1 cup granulated sugar

Chilled lemon-flavored sparkling water, as needed

1 small lemon, cut into thin slices and seeded, for garnish
   (optional)

1. Mix the cranberry juice, lemon juice, and orange juice together in a 1½-quart container. Whisk or briskly stir in the sugar and chill. This can be made and refrigerated up to 3 days ahead.

2. When ready to serve, fill tall glasses with ice, then add ⅓ to ½ cup (to your taste) of the cranberry medley. Top off with about the same amount of sparkling water. Garnish with a lemon slice, if desired.

➤ MAKES 8 TO 10 SERVINGS

Cran-Orange Lemonade plays well with others. To enjoy this with more potency, cut the sugar to $3/4$ cup. Serve by pouring a jigger of vodka, light rum, or tequila over the ice, then adding the base and sparkling water. You still want to maintain a 2-to-1 blend of sparkling water and base.

saturday's limeade

When I was growing up, Saturdays at my home meant that Dad was going to grill steaks and, more times than not, mix up some limeade. To this day, I believe limeade to be the most refreshing of beverages. Dad would say that I've "goosed this up a bit." I also think that something got added to Mom's and Dad's drinks.

2 cups water

1 1/2 cups granulated sugar

Grated zest of 2 limes

1 cup freshly squeezed lime juice (about 8 limes)

1/8 teaspoon kosher salt

Chilled lemon–lime soda or sparkling water, as needed

1. In a small saucepan, combine the water and sugar and bring to a boil, stirring to dissolve the sugar. Add the zest, cover, and remove from the heat. Let steep for 10 minutes. Strain through a fine-mesh strainer and let cool.

2. Pour the cooled sugar syrup into a 1-quart container. Add the lime juice and salt and stir to combine. Chill, covered, until very cold. This will keep for up to 1 week in the refrigerator or up to 1 year in the freezer.

3. When ready to serve, pour equal amounts of the lime concentrate and lemon-lime soda or sparkling water into a tall glass over lots of ice.

➤ MAKES 1 QUART CONCENTRATE, WHICH WILL YIELD ABOUT 8 SERVINGS

fresca refresher

Everything old seems to come back into vogue in cycles. Fresca has been around for a long time and is now being discovered by a new generation—or maybe baby boomers with more sophisticated tastes. The grapefruit-based soda marries skillfully with lemonade, and I highly recommend this tart and tangy sipper.

Cracked ice
1 quart freshly made lemonade, chilled
Three 12-ounce cans Fresca, chilled
1 lime, thinly sliced, for garnish

1. Fill 8 tall glasses with cracked ice. Add about $1/2$ cup of the lemonade to each glass.

2. Top each glass with Fresca (you will have some Fresca left over).

3. Garnish each glass with a lime slice and serve.

➤ MAKES 8 SERVINGS

french lemonade sparkler

The French have always captured our imagination when it comes to culinary expertise. In the past few years, gourmet food stores around the country have started selling carbonated French-style lemonade, which is not as sweet as our lemonade and much drier. This blend of American- and French-style lemonades is an excellent nonalcoholic apéritif for an adult summer gathering. Look for Lorina and Effervé sparkling French lemonades.

Cracked ice

1 quart freshly made lemonade, chilled

One 750-milliliter bottle imported French sparkling lemonade, chilled

Lemon wedges for garnish

1. Fill a tall glass with cracked ice. Fill it half full with the fresh lemonade, then top off with the French sparkling lemonade.

2. Garnish with a lemon wedge and serve.

➤ MAKES 8 TO 10 SERVINGS

The Italians and Portuguese also have sparkling lemon-flavored beverages. Depending on your locale, they might be easier to find, or you might like their flavor better in this concoction.

kiwi-lemonade spritzer

This lemonade is complex on the tongue and visually engaging. The flavors of the kiwifruit and lemon juice meld to produce a slightly sophisticated taste. With the black seeds of the kiwifruit, a muted green tone, and a brilliant strawberry atop the drink, well, you won't be able to resist this spritzer.

$^3/_4$ cup granulated sugar

6 kiwifruit, peeled and cut into pieces

2 cups freshly squeezed lemon juice (about 12 lemons)

1 cup water

Chilled water, sparkling water, or dry white wine, as needed

1 lime, cut into 8 wedges, for garnish (optional)

Sliced fresh strawberries for garnish (optional)

1. In a blender or food processor, process the sugar and kiwifruit until smooth.

2. In a 1-quart container, stir together the lemon juice and 1 cup water. Add the kiwifruit puree and stir. Chill until very cold.

3. To serve, pour $^1/_2$ cup of the kiwifruit mixture into at least a 10-ounce glass. Fill with ice and add roughly $^1/_2$ cup water, sparkling water, or wine to fill the glass. Place a lime wedge in each glass, if desired, and encourage folks to squeeze the lime. Garnish with strawberries, if desired.

➤ MAKES 8 SERVINGS

An easy way to peel a kiwifruit is to cut the fruit in half, then run a spoon between the peel and the fruit. It should come right out.

The wine option given is tricky. Make sure you taste the base and the wine you plan to use, making certain that they are compatible.

the new-fashioned lemonade

Things get a little wacky in this chapter. Included here are some lemonades you might never have thought of. Infusion lemonades have been the latest twist on this old-fashioned beverage, and I encourage you to try them. Don't be surprised when you see chocolate, maple syrup, and even lavender listed as ingredients. All bring a new dimension to an old favorite.

vanilla bean lemonade

Whether from Madagascar, Mexico, or Tahiti, vanilla has a mythical quality. I am a vanilla advocate. Vanilla can bring the subtlest of changes to many recipes. Here we'll take a shortcut, using frozen lemonade concentrate and enhancing the mix. Try using vanilla beans for an unadulterated vanilla essence.

> One 12-ounce can frozen lemonade concentrate, thawed
> 6 cups cold water
> $\frac{1}{3}$ cup granulated sugar
> $\frac{1}{4}$ teaspoon kosher salt
> 2 vanilla beans or pure vanilla extract to taste (start with 1 teaspoon)
> 2 large lemons, quartered and seeded

1. In a 2-quart container, combine the lemonade concentrate, water, sugar, and salt. Stir briskly until the sugar is dissolved.

2. If you are using vanilla beans, split the beans lengthwise down the middle and, using your fingers or a paring knife, scrape out the seeds. Add them to the lemonade mixture and stir until the seeds have separated. Let steep for 10 minutes or longer, depending on how much vanilla flavor you desire. If you are using vanilla extract, add it now.

3. Strain the lemonade, if desired, through a fine-mesh strainer to rid of any vanilla bean residue. Squeeze each lemon wedge into the container, adding the rinds as well.

4. Chill until very cold and serve in tall glasses over ice.

➤ MAKES 2 QUARTS

kaffir lime lemonade

This is one of the most interesting and certainly the most exotic recipe in the book. Kaffir limes are small, pear-shaped fruit, but the magic is in the leaves. A staple of the cuisines of Southeast Asia, dried or frozen leaves are usually available in most Asian food stores and in some health food stores. They are worth searching out, not only for this lemonade but also to give other dishes a mysterious flavor. Fresh kaffir lime leaves have an intense aroma that is clean and fresh, somewhat citrusy, and almost like a bouquet of flowers. The bay leaves add to the mystery of this lemonade by giving it a complex flavor.

$4^1/_2$ cups cold water
1 cup granulated sugar
4 fresh bay leaves or 2 dried
8 kaffir lime leaves
1 cup freshly squeezed lemon juice (about 6 lemons)
$^1/_2$ cup freshly squeezed lime juice (about 4 limes)

1. In a medium-size saucepan, combine $2^1/_2$ cups of the water, the sugar, bay leaves, and lime leaves. Bring to a gentle boil over medium heat, remove from the heat, cover, and let steep for 30 minutes.

2. Strain the mixture through a fine-mesh strainer into a 2-quart container. Stir in the lemon juice, lime juice, and remaining 2 cups water.

3. Chill until very cold and serve over ice.

➤ MAKES ABOUT 1$^1/_2$ QUARTS

pink lavender lemonade

Lavender is underrated as a flavoring agent in this country. We use it for all manner of bath soaps, house sprays, and massage oils, but this relaxing herb is a close relative of mint. The violet flowers of lavender add an intriguing astringency to all types of food. This lavender-infused lemonade is unique and well worth trying. It will transport you to the fields of Provence. Look for dried lavender flowers in gourmet and natural food stores and online at www.deananddeluca.com.

$4\frac{1}{2}$ cups cold water

1 tablespoon dried lavender flowers

$1\frac{1}{2}$ to $1\frac{3}{4}$ cups granulated sugar, depending on the sweetness of the strawberries

10 fresh strawberries, hulled and sliced

2 cups freshly squeezed lemon juice (about 12 lemons)

Sliced fresh strawberries for garnish (optional)

1. Place 2 cups of the water, the lavender, sugar, and strawberries in a medium-size saucepan and bring to a gentle boil over medium heat, stirring to dissolve the sugar. Reduce the heat to medium-low and simmer for 5 minutes. Cover, remove from the heat, and let steep for 10 minutes.

2. Strain the mixture through a fine-mesh strainer into a 2-quart container. Stir in the lemon juice and remaining $2\frac{1}{2}$ cups water.

3. Chill until very cold. Serve over ice, garnished with sliced strawberries if desired.

➤ MAKES ABOUT $1\frac{1}{2}$ QUARTS

mint-tea lemonade

No mint to be found, but you have a strong hankering for mint-flavored lemon-ade? This recipe is the ticket. It's the ultimate shortcut to a luxurious-tasting cooler. Using mint-flavored tea bags and refrigerated ready-made lemonade, it is basically fuss-free. You also can make this with fresh lemonade.

4 cups cold water

3 regular-size mint-flavored tea bags

$^3/_4$ to 1 cup granulated sugar, depending on the sweetness of the
   lemonade

1 quart freshly made or store-bought refrigerated lemonade

2 lemons, quartered and seeded

1. Bring 2 cups of the water to a gentle boil in a small saucepan. Add the tea bags, remove from the heat, cover, and let steep for 10 minutes.

2. Meanwhile, place the sugar in a 2-quart container. When the tea is ready, remove the tea bags without squeezing them, pour the tea over the sugar, and stir until the sugar is dissolved. Add the remaining 2 cups water. Let cool for 10 minutes. Pour in the lemonade, then squeeze the lemon wedges into the mixture. Put the rinds in, too. Stir to blend.

3. Chill until very cold and serve over ice.

➤ MAKES 2 QUARTS

meditation
lemonade

Delicate is a good way to describe this lemonade. Not that it's tart yet sweet, the way lemonade should taste. Instead, the individual flavors are muted, leaving one to wonder about its ingredients. Ready to relax? Try this drink.

1 cup granulated sugar

4 cups cold water

Finely grated zest of 1 orange

$1/4$ cup roughly chopped fresh spearmint leaves

1 cup freshly squeezed lemon juice (about 6 lemons)

$1/2$ cup freshly squeezed orange juice

Fresh mint sprigs for garnish (optional)

1. Combine the sugar and 2 cups of the water in a small saucepan. Bring to a gentle boil over medium heat, stirring to dissolve the sugar. Add the zest and mint, cover, remove from the heat, and let steep for about 15 minutes.

2. Strain the mixture through a fine-mesh strainer into a 2-quart container. Stir in the lemon juice, orange juice, and remaining 2 cups water until well blended.

3. Chill until very cold. Serve over ice, garnished with a mint sprig if desired.

➤ MAKES 1$1/2$ QUARTS

basil lemonade

The smell of fresh basil in late summer is intoxicating. Combining basil with another summer treat—lemonade—seems natural. The taste is definitely for an adult palate.

3 $\frac{1}{2}$ cups cold water

1 cup packed fresh basil leaves

$\frac{3}{4}$ cup granulated sugar

1 cup freshly squeezed lemon juice (about 6 lemons)

$\frac{1}{4}$ cup freshly squeezed lime juice (about 2 limes)

Small sprigs fresh basil for garnish (optional)

1. In a small saucepan, combine 2 cups of the water, the basil leaves, and sugar. Bring to a gentle boil over medium heat, stirring until the sugar is dissolved. Reduce the heat to medium-low, cover, and simmer for 5 minutes. Remove from the heat and let cool for about 30 minutes.

2. Strain through a fine-mesh strainer into a 1$\frac{1}{2}$-quart container. Add the lemon juice, remaining 1$\frac{1}{2}$ cups water, and lime juice and stir until well blended.

3. Chill until very cold. Serve over ice, garnished with a basil sprig if desired.

➤ MAKES ABOUT 1 QUART

The basil infusion can be made without the sugar, and refrigerated lemonade (homemade or store-bought) can be used in place of the 1$\frac{1}{2}$ cups water and lemon and lime juices, or just to taste. The infusion will keep for up to 3 days in the refrigerator. The addition of vodka makes for a nice cocktail.

citron
au chocolat

If lemon is a natural refresher and chocolate a mood elevator, why not combine the two? Don't say no until you've tried this. The chocolate flavor is not that pronounced. It mellows the lemonade and makes for a smooth, almost creamy, drink. This is a recipe where a frozen concentrate or refrigerated lemonade works equally well as freshly made.

1 $\frac{1}{2}$ quarts freshly made, reconstituted frozen concentrate or
   store-bought refrigerated lemonade
1 cup chocolate syrup, such as Fox's U-Bet or Hershey's
Chocolate shavings for garnish (optional)

1. In a 2-quart container, mix the lemonade and chocolate syrup together.

2. Chill until very cold. Serve over ice, sprinkled with chocolate shavings if desired.

➤ MAKES 1 $\frac{3}{4}$ QUARTS

Chocolate shavings are easily created by running a vegetable peeler over a room temperature block or bar of chocolate. Use semi-sweet chocolate or, for a special taste, gianduja, a Swiss hazelnut-flavored chocolate.

new england lemonade

Use maple syrup in lemonade? This lemonade has a slightly nutty flavor without hiding the citrus tones that make lemonade lemonade. Trust me, this will surprise you.

> 1 cup pure maple syrup
> $^3/_4$ cup freshly squeezed lemon juice (about 4 $^1/_2$ lemons)
> $^1/_2$ cup freshly squeezed lime juice (about 4 limes)
> $^1/_8$ teaspoon kosher salt
> 6 cups cold water

1. In a 2-quart container, combine the maple syrup, lemon juice, lime juice, and salt and stir to blend well. Add the water and stir again.

2. Chill until very cold and serve over ice.

➤ MAKES 2 QUARTS

ginger-infused lemonade

In case you have forgotten, ginger equals spicy heat. This one's for taste buds that can handle anything. Drink this lemonade very cold.

6 cups cold water

$^{1}/_{2}$ cup peeled and roughly chopped fresh ginger

$^{1}/_{2}$ cup honey

$^{1}/_{2}$ cup freshly squeezed lemon juice (about 3 lemons)

$^{1}/_{4}$ cup freshly squeezed orange juice

1. In a small saucepan, bring 2 cups of the water to a boil. Add the ginger and honey, cover, remove from the heat, and let steep for 30 minutes.

2. Strain the mixture through a fine-mesh strainer into a 2-quart container, pressing on the solids. Pour in the lemon and orange juices and stir to combine. Add the remaining 4 cups water and stir again to combine.

3. Chill until very cold and serve over ice.

➤ MAKES 2 QUARTS

An easy and safe way to peel ginger is with a spoon.

lemonade milkshake

This is a crazy recipe, but a fun one. Long gone, Edward's Drugstore in Greensboro, North Carolina, made something similar to this, and if I got good grades, I was treated to a glass. That was way too many years ago, and this version is updated and much healthier.

> 2 cups lowfat milk
> 1 pint lowfat vanilla yogurt, softened
> One 6-ounce can frozen lemonade concentrate, thawed
> 1 pint lemon sorbet, softened

1. In a blender, combine the milk, yogurt, and lemonade concentrate. First pulse, then process until smooth.

2. Divide the mixture between 4 tall glasses and top with a large scoop of the lemon sorbet. Serve immediately.

➤ MAKES 4 SERVINGS

cucumber lemonade

Remember the expression "cool as a cucumber"? Although cucumber lemonade may sound strange, it is very refreshing. When I was growing up in the South, we would regularly combine cucumbers with sweetened acids and serve them as a summer side dish.

> 1 seedless English cucumber, peeled and cut in half
> 2 quarts freshly made, reconstituted frozen concentrate or store-
>   bought refrigerated lemonade

1. In a small mixing bowl, grate the cucumber. Let stand for 30 minutes.

2. Strain the cucumber and add the liquid to the lemonade. Or dump both the cucumber pulp and the juice into the lemonade.

3. Chill until very cold and serve over ice.

➤ MAKES 2 QUARTS

lemonade
with
adult
flavors

Lemonade really does play well with others, making it the perfect mixer for all sorts of alcoholic drinks. From beer to wine, lemonade finds a starring role. Many of these drinks can be made without the spirits, giving them a life at many a party. In either guise, these lemonades also can enhance just plain kicking-back times.

wicked pink lady lemonade

If you order a pink lady in a bar, one of two types might show up at your table. One has gin, cream, and grenadine, the other an egg white and lemon juice. I propose a compromise and take the best from both. Gin is the component that holds this drink together, so use a good label. If you wish, replace the grenadine with cranberry juice cocktail.

1 1/2 ounces good-quality gin
1/2 cup freshly made lemonade
Dash of grenadine or splash of cranberry juice cocktail
2 teaspoons heavy cream

1. In a cocktail shaker or jar with a lid, combine the gin, lemonade, grenadine or cranberry juice cocktail, and cream. Add ice and shake until chilled and frothy.

2. Strain into a champagne or martini glass and serve.

➤ MAKES 1 DRINK

To make a pitcher for guests, combine 2/3 cup gin, 2 cups lemonade, 1 to 2 teaspoons grenadine or 1 tablespoon cranberry juice cocktail, and 1/2 cup heavy cream in a blender. Blend until frothy, then serve over ice. Makes 4 drinks.

slush puppy deluxe

Imagine a hot, sweltering, humid day. Then imagine the coolest of ways to quench your thirst. If you have this stuff in the freezer, you are prepared to beat the heat.

$4\frac{1}{2}$ cups cold water

2 regular-size tea bags

1 cup granulated sugar

One 12-ounce can frozen lemonade concentrate, thawed

One 12-ounce can frozen orange juice concentrate, thawed

1 cup dark rum

Chilled lemon-lime soda, as needed

1. Bring 1 cup of the water to a boil in a small saucepan. Add the tea bags, cover, remove from the heat, and let steep for 10 to 15 minutes. You want a strong tea. Remove the tea bags without squeezing them and let the tea cool. This can be made a day in advance.

2. Combine the sugar and remaining $3\frac{1}{2}$ cups water in a small saucepan and bring to a boil over medium heat, stirring to dissolve the sugar. Remove from the heat, cover, and let cool.

3. Pour the tea, sugar syrup, and lemonade and orange juice concentrates into a 5-quart Dutch oven. Add the rum and stir until blended. Place in the freezer. After about 1 hour, stir the mixture. Do that once more, then allow the mixture to firm up.

4. To serve, spoon about $\frac{3}{4}$ cup of the slush into an old-fashioned glass. Top with the soda, stirring until slushy. Return the remainder of the mixture to the freezer and use as needed.

➤ MAKES ABOUT 2 QUARTS, ENOUGH FOR A WEEK AT THE BEACH

fuzzy peach lemonade

One of the hazards of living near someone who develops recipes is that you are asked to taste food in the early stages of development (that is, bad food). Sometimes having game neighbors gives you that final inspiration that makes a recipe work. So thanks, Barry and Robin, for being such great guinea pigs and suggesting the schnapps. And, yes, this lemonade will make you fuzzy.

6 medium-size, very ripe peaches, peeled, pitted, and cut into chunks
1 cup granulated sugar
2 cups cold water
2 cups freshly squeezed lemon juice (about 12 lemons)
2 cups peach schnapps, or to taste

1. In a food processor or blender, pulse the peaches and sugar until blended, then process until smooth. Add the water and pulse to combine.

2. Strain the peach mixture through a fine-mesh strainer into a 1 1/2-quart container, pressing on the solids to extract as much juice as possible. Add the lemon juice and stir to combine. Add the peach schnapps and stir again to combine.

3. Chill until very cold and serve over ice.

➤ MAKES 1 1/2 QUARTS

This lemonade made without the peach schnapps and mixed with an equal amount of Cabernet Sauvignon is very tasty. Thinking I was nuts, I consulted my copy of *Mr. Boston Official Bartender's Guide*, and there was lemonade made with 2 ounces of claret per drink. There are many wines that could turn this lemonade into your "house special."

lemonade summer wine cooler

The inspiration for this recipe came from the late Jenny Fitch, who, with her husband, R.B., set out to create a perfect retreat near Chapel Hill, North Carolina—The Fearrington House. National acclaim has been loud and frequent for the inn and restaurant. This is a reworked version of their lemon balm cooler. I always have trouble finding lemon balm and a few other ingredients, so I worked around them. The result is a notch or two away from the real thing, but this version has satisfied many a folk at my house.

2 cups water
$^1/_2$ cup granulated sugar
Grated zest of 1 lemon
3 regular-size blackberry- or black currant–flavored tea bags
$^3/_4$ cup freshly squeezed lemon juice (about 4 $^1/_2$ lemons)
One 750-milliliter bottle white wine
Fresh blackberries for garnish (optional)

1. Combine the water, sugar, and zest in a medium-size saucepan and bring to a gentle boil, stirring to dissolve the sugar. Add the tea bags, remove from the heat, cover, and let steep for 10 minutes. Remove the tea bags without squeezing them, strain the syrup through a fine-mesh strainer, and let cool.

2. Combine the blackberry tea, lemon juice, and wine in a 1 $^1/_2$-quart container.

3. Chill until very cold. Serve in punch cups or champagne glasses, garnished with blackberries if desired.

➤ MAKES 1 $^1/_2$ QUARTS

rum runner's lemonade

This is a fun summer party drink that can be served over ice or put in a blender with ice and frozen. If you wish to leave out the rum, replace it with club soda.

One 10-ounce can frozen tropical fruit mixer concentrate. thawed

One 12-ounce can frozen lemonade concentrate. thawed

$4^{1}/_{2}$ cups cold water

$1^{1}/_{2}$ cups dark rum

1. In a $2^{1}/_{2}$-quart container, combine the fruit mixer concentrate, lemonade concentrate, water, and rum. Stir to blend.

2. Serve over ice, or put 1 cup in a blender with ice and blend until the drink becomes slushy. Serve immediately.

➤ MAKES 2 QUARTS

blue lagoon

If only the color of this libation could transport me to a blue lagoon. I guess consuming enough of it could. Tread lightly with this bartender's favorite: it goes down very smoothly. This drink is a takeoff on the martini. Although it is usually served in a stemmed glass, any glass will do.

1 1/2 ounces vodka
1 ounce blue curaçao
1/3 cup freshly made lemonade

1. In a cocktail shaker or any jar with a lid (a Mason jar works great), combine the vodka, blue curaçao, and lemonade. Add ice and shake until cold.

2. Strain into an oversize martini glass or serve on the rocks in a highball glass.

➤ MAKES 1 DRINK

To enhance the lemon flavor, use lemon-flavored vodka. Also try substituting lemon-flavored rum.

celebration lemonade

Mother's Day, a bridal luncheon, or graduation calls for something special. The base of this lemonade can be made a day or two ahead. Using the base gives you flexibility to please those who don't care for wine, as well as allowing you to protect the kids.

$^3/_4$ cup plus 2 tablespoons granulated sugar

1 cup water

$^1/_3$ cup fresh mint leaves, preferably peppermint

2 pints fresh strawberries, hulled

1 cup freshly squeezed lemon juice (about 6 lemons)

One 750-milliliter bottle dry sparkling wine or an equal amount of
   water (about 1 quart), chilled

---

1. In a small saucepan, combine $^3/_4$ cup of the sugar, the water, and mint and bring to a boil over medium heat, stirring to dissolve the sugar. Remove from the heat, cover, and let steep for 15 to 20 minutes, letting the mint infuse the sugar syrup. Strain the mint-infused syrup through a fine-mesh strainer and let cool for another 10 minutes.

2. Meanwhile, in a blender or food processor, process the strawberries and the remaining 2 tablespoons sugar until smooth.

3. In a 1$^1/_2$-quart container, combine the strawberry puree and lemon juice. Add the mint syrup and stir. Chill until very cold.

4. When ready to serve, divide the strawberry-lemon base equally among 8 to 10 champagne glasses. Top with the sparkling wine and serve.

➤ MAKES 8 TO 10 SERVINGS

Only sparkling wines from the Champagne region of France can legally be called Champagne, and these French wines can get expensive. Try California sparkling wine instead. One of the best values in sparkling wines are the *cavas* from Spain.

california lemonade

I was introduced to this lemonade on a trip to the Napa Valley. After touring wineries all day (and, of course, sampling), a tart whiskey tasted mighty good.

2 ounces sour mash whiskey

Juice of 1 lemon (about 3 tablespoons)

Juice of 1 lime (about 2 tablespoons)

1 tablespoon confectioners' sugar

$1/4$ teaspoon grenadine

Cracked ice, as needed

Chilled club soda, as needed

1. Put the sour mash, lemon and lime juices, sugar, and grenadine in a cocktail shaker or any glass jar with a lid. Add the cracked ice and shake for about 30 seconds, until very cold.

2. Strain into a 10-ounce glass and fill with club soda.

➤ MAKES 1 DRINK

tuscan thyme lemonade

On a recent evening at Beppe, a hot new Tuscan restaurant in New York City, a special cocktail was offered—thyme-infused lemonade. It was a perfect predinner cocktail and also worked with the robust Tuscan food. With a little begging, the waitperson finally told me the ingredients. Using that as a starting point, I came up with my own version of that cocktail.

1 cup granulated sugar
4 1/2 cups cold water
3 sprigs fresh thyme
1 1/2 cups freshly squeezed lemon juice (about 9 lemons)
9 ounces Absolut Citron vodka
6 ounces Cuarenta y Tres (an herb-infused liqueur)
Lemon wedges for garnish (optional)
Fresh thyme sprigs for garnish (optional)

1. In a small saucepan, combine the sugar and 1 cup of the water. Bring to a gentle boil over medium heat, stirring to dissolve the sugar. Reduce the heat to medium-low and simmer for 3 minutes. Add the thyme sprigs, remove from the heat, cover, and let steep for 10 to 15 minutes, depending on your fondness for thyme. Strain and let cool completely.

2. In a 1 1/2-quart container, combine the thyme-infused syrup, lemon juice, and remaining 3 1/2 cups water until well blended. Chill until very cold.

3. To serve, fill six 10-ounce glasses with ice and pour 1 1/2 ounces of the vodka and 1 ounce of the liqueur into each glass. Top off with the lemonade and stir. Garnish with a lemon wedge and/or a thyme sprig, if desired.

➤ MAKES 6 SERVINGS

lemonade comfort

Southerners take some abuse for our love of Southern Comfort. I suspect it's because many carpetbagger college students drank way too much when they were studying at our fine Southern institutions of higher learning. Southern Comfort does comfort you as you sip the brown elixir. And gussied up with lemonade and champagne, the drink is sublime. A perfect beverage to welcome guests into your home.

1 1/2 cups freshly made lemonade

1/2 cup Southern Comfort, chilled

1/4 cup freshly squeezed orange juice

1/4 cup freshly squeezed lime juice (about 2 limes)

One 750-milliliter bottle champagne, chilled

Lemon twists for garnish (optional)

Fresh mint sprigs for garnish (optional)

1. Pour the lemonade into a 2-quart container. Add the Southern Comfort, orange juice, and lime juice and stir to blend. Chill until very cold.

2. When ready to serve, add the champagne slowly and stir just to combine. You don't want to stir away the bubbles. Pour into chilled stemmed glasses and garnish with the lemon twists and mint sprigs, if desired.

➤ MAKES 8 SERVINGS

shandy

Hard lemonades abound in the beer sections of our local stores. The English have been combining lemonade and beer for centuries. In traditional English style, they kept it simple.

1 part beer
1 part freshly made lemonade

Slowly fill a frosted glass or beer mug halfway with beer. Top off with an equal amount of lemonade. Stir, if desired.

➤ THIS CAN SERVE ANY NUMBER

lemonade martini

With the popularity of martinis, I just had to include one. This martini, like all martinis, is simple to make. The trick is working that cocktail shaker until the drink is ice-cold. Serve this in sugar-rimmed martini glasses.

1 cup lemon-flavored vodka
$^1/_2$ cup freshly made lemonade
Cracked ice
4 thin lemon slices for garnish

1. In a cocktail shaker or a jar with a lid, combine the vodka, lemonade, and as much ice as you can get in the shaker. Shake until very cold.

2. Strain the mixture into sugar-rimmed martini glasses and float a thin lemon slice on top.

➤ MAKES 4 SERVINGS

To coat the rims of your glasses, place a small amount of water or Karo corn syrup in a small bowl that is big enough for the rim of a martini glass to fit into. Put several tablespoons of granulated sugar in another small bowl. Dip the rim of each glass into the liquid, then into the sugar.

lynchburg lemonade

John Edgerton, a Southern scholar and writer, once proclaimed to a group of Southern food enthusiasts, "I have a White Lily [flour] body and a Jack Daniel's soul." I suspect many a Southerner could express that sentiment. Jack Daniel's is as much a part of Southern culture as grits. In fact, Lynchburg Lemonade was created to help those who needed something other than branch water to help pour Old No. 7 into their souls. Most mixologists use Triple Sec, but I believe that Mr. Daniel deserves the richness and depth of Grand Marnier. Either will work. Some versions don't use lemonade, but this one stays true to the classic and its name.

Cracked ice, as needed

2 ounces Jack Daniel's Black Label Sour-Mash whiskey or other suitable whiskey

2 ounces Grand Marnier

2 ounces of your favorite lemonade

2 ounces (roughly) carbonated citrus-flavored soda or club soda

Sprigs fresh mint and long-stemmed maraschino cherries for garnish (optional)

1. Fill a tall 10-ounce glass with cracked ice.

2. Add the Jack Daniel's, Grand Marnier, and lemonade. Top off with the citrus-flavored soda or, for a less sweet version, use the club soda.

3. Garnish with mint and cherries, if desired.

➤ MAKES 1 SERVING

seduction

My father's generation is said to have "found its thrill on Blueberry Hill," and by using a few blueberries, some ginger, and amaretto, this lemonade could lead to your own "thrill." Blueberries fall into that class of berries that chase away the bad stuff that builds up in our bodies, and ginger has long been suspected of being an aphrodisiac. And amaretto is the Italians' "love elixir." Put the three together, marry them with lemonade, and you have one sexy drink. This would be great for a Valentine's Day party.

2 cups water

$1/2$ cup granulated sugar, or to taste

4 quarter-size slices peeled ginger about $1/4$-inch thick

1 cup fresh or frozen blueberries

1 cup of your favorite lemonade

1 cup amaretto

1. Pour the water into a 1-quart saucepan and add the sugar and ginger slices. Bring the water to a boil, reduce the heat to low, and simmer for 10 minutes, stirring until the sugar is dissolved. Remove from the heat and let cool.

2. Place the blueberries in a food processor and process until smooth. Set aside.

3. Remove the ginger slices from the sugar syrup. Combine the ginger-infused sugar syrup, lemonade, and amaretto in a container and chill until needed.

4. To serve, chill stemmed glasses, such as martini or champagne glasses. Fill the glasses almost full with the lemonade mixture, then add a tablespoon of the blueberry puree to each glass. Let the puree combine with the lemonade without any help from you. Serve and watch out.

➤ MAKES 4 SERVINGS, BUT KEEPS REFRIGERATED FOR UP TO A WEEK

I

about the author

Photograph by KAT

Fred Thompson is a food stylist, writer, and recipe developer who trained at the Culinary Institute of America. He lives in New York City and Raleigh, North Carolina, where he writes "The Weekend Gourmet" column for the *News & Observer*. He is also the author of *Iced Tea*.

acknowledgments

To Pam Hoenig, an editor who changed my life's direction on January 21. To Susan Byrnes for great photographs, when her life was changed on September 11, and Justin Schwartz. To Toni Allegro, who helps me look good on the page. To Marty Umans. To Elizabeth Van Itallie for the kicking design of both my books. To all the *great* folks at the Harvard Common Press. To my English professor aunt, Dr. Janice Thompson: see, some things did stick! To Linda Johnson, who always thought I had a book in me. And finally, to my computer expert and proofreader, Kat, who let me go insane when necessary.